M.L. ELDER

PROPERTY OF THE UNIVERSE

The Book of Nos and other Disembodied Poetics

HOLLYWOOD BROTHERHOOD CO.

PROPERTY OF THE UNIVERSE
The Book of Nos and other Disembodied Poetics
All Rights Reserved.
Copyright © 2023 M.L. Elder
v3.0

This is a work of poeticized fiction. The opinions expressed in this manuscript are solely the opinions of the author and do not represent the opinions or thoughts of the publisher. The author has represented and warranted full ownership and/or legal right to publish all the materials in this book.

This book may not be reproduced, transmitted, or stored in whole or in part by any means, including graphic, electronic, or mechanical without the express written consent of the publisher except in the case of brief quotations embodied in critical articles and reviews.

Hollywood Brotherhood Co.

ISBN: 978-0-578-27405-8

Library of Congress Control Number: 2022919428

Cover Photo © 2023 M.L. Elder. All rights reserved - used with permission.

PRINTED IN THE UNITED STATES OF AMERICA

PROPERTY OF THE UNIVERSE

The Book of Nos and other
Disembodied Poetics

I.

The Book of Love

II.

Meet Pos-Pis
for Pregnant Moms

III.

God Strikes
My Sister

IV.

Closing Thoughts
Based on Closing Blessing

I.

The Book of Nos

Nos and Robot: Beyond the Singularity & Betting on the Messenger
and other Disembodied Poetics

by M.L. Elder

Dedicated to Sinclair, Sherry, and Worasanan for your generosity and kindness to a very special cat for so many bright years...

Thank You.

**1 -
Prologue:**

**NOS AND ROBOT
BEYOND THE SINGULARITY &
BETTING ON THE MESSENGER**

the mountain god (Sanshin)
the guardian of villages,
   providing security and peace.

      the denizen god
      the heavenly god,
      the mountain god

acting as number one
   the earthly god, this mountain spirit.

appearing to the mortal realm
as a wise old warrior
accompanied by
   his messenger, a fearless tiger

with unlimited knowledge
of all kingdoms—

  (god, human, and animal).

but, this begs the question…
   who is the real supreme entity here,
   and who is actually the companion?

**2 -
Earth:**

you can never be too careful
in this cold, dark world

> a black coat
> a pale blue dot
> and a suit of work

  fringe.

enter alone
 fly alone
find a navigator

find a home.

**3 -
Pilot:**

the sky is calling

the old wasp—
   ripped from bonds
      dragged into thick air

beside you
an empty seat,
a throne

black leather boots
  and nobody home.

8 -
Battle:

returning
home—

he is there
fighting stillness

      fighting hard.

we rushed to the well
we tried, everything

life in fragments,
    is still.life

on the boat
he puts his head down
on my arm, and we sail

   to nowhere special
       together.

and then there were three,
  three soft jewels of time

happiness, floating
  toward nothing special

again.
 we battle
again.

9 -
War:

leaving
  returning
    and resting

on eternal distant shores.

he was,
  always there

on the wind-worn cliffs
of desolate western waters

    a lighthouse beacon.

we think about
people, and things
  at night; in rough seas

how hard it is to balance two lives
across two worlds, between
three veils—

into the shadows
and darkness
he steps
away

    good-bye.

10 -
Cambria:

   it wasn't easy
nothing was ever easy

but, this was harder
than the hardest
not easy thing
he had ever
done

    it was the only way.

from the beginning
you're bonded

from the beginning
you're posted

from the beginning
you're routed

    alternate routes
through possibilities

   it was the only way
from the beginning.

   honor can be satisfied,
"Where are your people now?"

      he was gone.

**11 -
Sea:**

over and done…
  unmistakably, quite dead.

each seemed more sad and alone
                          now

    if there was anyone helping
    it was not apparent
    that day

he pulled the bag
out of his pocket
and

p o u r e d it over the rocks
into the ocean surf
   b e l o w

"I have died of my own hand."
     he whispered to the sky
                       in anger

each seemed more sad and alone
                          now

over and done…
  unmistakably, quite dead.

20 -
Sirius A:

holding our bags
nothing but empty
    shores

sand and
crushing
    empty waves

we board
our starship
    again

  re-form
re.form.ation

we set forth
for a sea of
nations

      yet unknown
  and

 floating
all alone

out—
amongst
the pinpricked black.

21 -
Ulas j1342+0928:

there was a storm
there's always a storm

solar winds rage
      the plan
   the written
page

it isn't worth much
 in times of
    intense
        interstellar
           struggle.

the internal lights
were all we had

   sparkling campfire embers

there was no
   barrier between
night and day

   he shook his head.
there was nothing there
save a savior

"It's a disgrace."
    it really was

  we should go
do you fancy coming
           along?

22 -
Trappist-1:

a discovery
     deep beneath the ground

first
  droplets of water

this world
     is full of
flickering promise

   defining
        the
           darkness

  and finally

they were standing there
at our perimeter,
  perspective

energy in form
 surrounded
  by huge

quantum shells

  they stare at him,
and pass

without a word
  we go inside.

23 -
Cl j1001+0220:

"Now, you say sorry…"

   there's infinite
     more work

mouthpiece,

     nobody was fooled.

somewhere nearby
 and behind

he was doing his best,
immutable music
flashed forward

  with
deep-set eyes

*"Would you happen to have
any thoughts on the approach?"*

   what
     we need is
    an interface

 across boundaries.of
holographic culture

*"A way to let them know
through higher
symbolism."*

**28 -
Mizar:**

with a little pressure
    we illuminated the background night

with computer code
  and knowledge

        a new purpose
             in art—

teaching life
  to evolve

on the grandest scale,
this cosmic grandeur

spread from world
        to new world

    by a pilot
    turned deity,
    and a sphynx
    turned messenger tiger.

29 - Sweeps-04:

seeing is believing!

   and
   when we were finished

the goal
  never known,
     finally

revealed
the gallery.

     catalogued,
  a collection of

worlds ablaze
with consciousness

     expanding
en.light.enment

a universal museum
     sitting on a bead of mercury

  the exhibition, at last.

30 -
Epilogue:

Art & Muse.um A3104+
Beyond the Singular.ity
Update V2.Nos

one day
we will paint our way
across the stars
with computronium
a pilot and navigator
a messenger and light bearer
from sirius a to ulas j1342+0928
trappist-1 to cl j1001+0220
aldebaran to gn-z11
alcor b to sdss j1229+1122
mizar to sweeps-04
and when you look
out across our heavens
from world to new world
you will see our pulpit
the enlightenment
of each new world
hanging there
suspended
at the zero-point
bringing light to darkness
in the ever expanding
limitless galactic
museum of
universal
consciousness

       - ME > A-3104.ME // 01.19.2018
       - NOS > A-3104.1.NOS // 10.12.2021

Nos & Robot
Artwork and Plan
by James Stone & Mikal Elder

PROPERTY OF THE UNIVERSE

II.

New PoeTRY for Pyrotechnicians
and other Disembodied Poetics

by M.L. Elder

*Dedicated to James Grauerholz, with whom
I once shot Hunter's .454 Casull Magnum,
sat in Jack's "favorite" old chair, and
held Bill's secret crystal revolver...*

For all that inspiration, after all these years, still.

    Thank You.

Denizens

Let me tell you something about life:
As with all truly perilous journeys,
this one begins with a cat.

Nos and I —

> *"I learned a long time ago that war is easier than real life."*

I met this guy once... he said that our only hope was in the stars. I believed him then, but now I understand him. As a species, we have a lot to never learn.

> *"The deeper and darker the pit, the brighter the light we need to light it."*

A.lien fish can fill itself with food that has helium inside to where, if it does well and catches/eats a lot, it floats up and out and cannot breathe, and dies — all in moderation, on this world or any...

Title: BLACK BADGE

Make no mistake about the actual order of things...
fully-formed eggs always come first, and chickens
only start to evolve after cracks begin to form...

The universe is a massive
organic computer,
a grand movie,
and
we mirror the echo
of lives we have always lived,
in repetitive circles of time,
as the stage revolves
around the scenery.

All animals extinct
Now humans are the last –
the end of the endangered species list
Recording log, not sure why
     or for whom anymore, before 900th void walk

Merging of quantum mechanics and general
relativity gave us answers, but not the answers we
expected or were prepared for

Alone, we were always alone, sometimes
monitored, but eventually forgotten, an entire
universe of lost toys

Shrunken down,
to one last outpost,
almost nothing.

A Rise In Violence

The unexpected evolution of timeless and seemingly disassociated fates — from a business savvy saloon girl in the late 1800's gold rush days of Northern Nevada, a degenerate gambler caught up in the seedy mafia underbelly of 1970's Las Vegas, and a mysterious old philosopher gunsmith whose relationships seem oddly out of step with the changing world, circa 1994 — all come together in unexpected ways to influence a young errand boy in his life-and-death struggle with a scrupulous casino executive tied to organized crime in modern day Sin City.

Sigma Sammy / A Rise in Violence

Sigma Sammy
Based on True Events
1985, Downtown Las Vegas

Addiction management is the number one preoccupation of the human beast. Once you understand that, my friend, you have the necessary knowledge to make or break any institution in this world. Sammy Depalma-Brown, 1985, walking through the main lobby of the Riviera with three million dollars in a duffle bag over his left shoulder. He had just used his knowledge of human addiction to leverage a favor from a junky employee in the cage, a man who had clearly let his addictions compromise his better position. Sammy had already bailed this piece of human waste out, more than a few times, with some of the less-than-understanding business men here in town, and now he was calling the cards he had saved in his hip pocket. That's how this game is played, if you want to be a serious player. Are you following me? Yes? So, this junky lets Sam convince him to leave the cage unlocked and take a quick emergency shit in the restroom just around the corner, as a favor to get him back to even with Sam, and the junky did it because he was addicted to the junk, but he was even more addicted to knowing that Sam had the connections to hold off the sharks circling his junky debts all red and bloody in the water. Once an addict is down, and behind the curve, there is no way to get level again, except for getting bailed out, and this was the price of Sammy bailing him out. So, he didn't ask a single fucking question, and he took his coordinated shit with the cage unlocked, which bought Sam access to the main cash drawer up front and approximately seven minutes of alarm-free time to stroll right out the front doors with nobody the wiser. In those days, casinos downtown would go down to one cage attendant between 4 to 7AM to save money, because the only people left on the casino floor at those hours are the drunks and the hardcore degenerate gamblers. But, what Sammy also knew was that they didn't collect the night's take until 9AM the morning after, so when do you think Sammy asked fuck-o to take his extremely important shit? Right you are, 5AM on the dot, after everybody had gone home and the floor was scattered with nothing but minimal riff-raff. So, as you're starting to see, Sammy had improved his life situation significantly with some minimal technical competence, by understanding the casino floor, by knowing the business of addiction, and by reading the tells of the human condition. And, brother, it worked like a charm. Sammy was in and out of that cash drawer in about two minutes flat, not distracted by anything, in the cage and right out, with a gym bag full of cold cash, like butter on hot biscuits. And, son, I want you to think real hard before you answer this next question... What do you think happened between the cage and the front door of that casino, as Sammy strolled out with his well-earned take? I'll tell you what happened. A bigger fish pulled a bigger con. Let me clarify that. You see, Sammy, while smarter than the average bear, was still human. Sammy wasn't above the trappings that we are all susceptible to. You and me too kid, don't think I don't recognize that. Sammy drank, Sammy used to beat on his broads a little, and Sammy definitely liked the Sports Book.

Why do you think he needed that three mil, anyway? So, no guards stopped Sammy. No movie chase through the streets and alleyways ensued, no car chase with thirty cop cars in tow, no Wild West gun fight started in the lobby and spilled out onto the Vegas strip. No. What happened was just another example of perfect exploitation of the human condition — Addiction. You see, Sammy may have occasionally hit the bottle a little heavy, he may have bet on a few bad horses and then went home and took it out on his old lady, but the one thing Sammy never compromised was his love for his ma. Sammy, for all the gangster he was, was still a momma's boy. And, what you probably don't realize was that a large portion of that 3 mil take would have gone straight to ma, even before it went to any other debts or calls. So, there's Sammy, strolling through the Riviera lobby, pretty happy with himself for pulling all this together, and what does he see just off the left side of the main lobby doors? The Sigma Derby horse race machine. Man, at the time this thing was state-of-the-art, fully automated, mechanical horses that never missed a beat and ran all night long, a real shiny wet dream under glass for a guy like Sammy. But, here's the kicker, not only did it catch his eye from the perspective of his Sports Book habit, it also fulfilled his most important addiction of all, because the casino had just re-advertised that machine with a chance to win a big new Cadillac DeVille, if you could parlay enough long-shots into a trifecta win on a main race, essentially like hitting a jackpot on a major slot. And, the Caddy they had put on display in the lobby to attract attention, due to the fact that there was a Red Hat Women's Convention in town the week prior, was a big bright pink boat, looked just like a huge metal pink flamingo, and something any Italian mother would love. And, Sammy, being the momma's boy he was, and feeling pretty good about his current luck with money, and being addicted to sports betting, and even more addicted to taking care of his ma, decided to play it cool and throw a few quarters at that machine in passing. And, he did. And, on his first race, he ran the ticket and won the fucking crown with three of the most lame-duck, broken down, worthless, stag horses in the stable to pick from. I mean, winning this race was probably comparable to winning the very worst statistical bet on the entire Las Vegas Strip on the first fucking try. Won't happen again in a billion trys, type-of-win. So, of course, all the bells and whistles start going off, and all the people on the floor all come running to see the commotion, and the slot attendants and floor manager all respond, and the casino comes alive again, at 5:05AM. And, Sammy is standing there, at the center of all that attention, with a bag full of three million in stolen money and about two more minutes left before his time runs out on that cage alarm. And, he's there, because the casino is the best in this world at exploiting the mathematics of addiction. A bigger fish, and a bigger con. And so, Sammy's addictions were also his downfall, same old story. He simply got distracted. So, when Sammy tried to leave without his legitimately won new Caddy, the small early morning mob of onlookers and casino employees wouldn't have it. They thought he was confused, or overwhelmed, or something. By that time the door alarm for the cage had tripped, and when security responded they found an empty cage and an empty money drawer, and the junky, well that retard was still in the washroom, literally taking the shit Sammy told him to take. So, when Sammy, with that alarm clock running in his head, finally tried to make an honest break for it, the idiot onlookers mobbed that son-of-a-bitch, happy for him, congratulating him feverishly, and keeping him right there, clear up until the moment when the casino security team finally put 1 and 1 together and went and arrested him. Undone by addiction, good luck with bad timing, and addiction. He should have just walked when he had the chance. And, that's the eternal story of the human race, kid. We never know when to stop feeding the beast and just walk the fuck away. Am I right? So, the final part of this story, that you don't know yet, is how Sammy knew so much about the workings of the casino and the cage. See, Sammy was one of my employees, and an OK guy, and he was pretty damn smart, and I knew how valuable that is in a business associate, and I still know Sammy's ma very well, and all that made my decision very very hard. Was it fair for this guy to be arrested? And to suffer the public shame of all that goes along with that shit? In addition to losing all his money and his future employability? Arrested? Naw, not for a guy like Sammy. That ship had sailed long ago, my friend. As a show of compassion and understanding, on our parts, we just decided to let Sammy and his junky bathroom friend move on to better things. You understand me? Now, I know Sammy's ma misses him. And, I know she wonders where he ran off to. Maybe she thinks he made another score and ran off to keep it all for himself. Maybe she thinks he ran off to the Bahamas with some cooze and left his his poor old ma alone to rot away on Hoover Ave, which is a horrible thing for a mother to have to think about her own son, but it's better than the alternative. Because the truth is, Sammy and that fuckin' junky friend of his are both still scuba diving in Lake Mead, together, all these years later. But, why would I tell you that, eh? Because, son, sitting here, looking at you, seeing those tracks on your fucking arms and the white bags under your red eyes, I know, I know almost everything I need to know, without you saying a single solitary word. Almost. Someday, kid, your demons are going to catch up to you, get the better of you. And, when they do, a man like me will come calling when you least expect it. It's the chemistry of addiction mixed with the mathematics of business, and if there's one thing that we both know, it's that you understand chemistry. And if there's a second thing that we both now know, due to our mutual understanding of the unraveling of Sammy's little heist, it's that nothing good comes from unnecessary distractions when you're already ahead of the curve. So, the question becomes, kid, look at me, has your ship already sailed? Why are you here now? Did you get distracted? Why didn't you walk when you had the chance? Addiction? Same old human story? Has your addiction now compromised your better position kid? Look, junk and our thing - business - don't work together, it just don't. It don't mix well, it's like vinegar and olive oil, associated, maybe, but no matter what you do, still separate. Kid, you should have walked when you had the chance, when you were ahead. But, you didn't. It's human nature. So, look at me son. Clean yourself up. Be a man. Show some poise here, some of that Roman backbone. Those are our people. Romans, warriors, Italians. We are what's left of their empire. This is a very pivotal moment for you, in your life, in the rest of your life. Now, I'm only going to ask you this question one single time, so listen very very carefully to every fucking word...

Where. Is. My. Fucking. Money?

Horseshoes / A Rise in Violence

1885 - Western
    Delilah the Dove (1871-1942 / 71)
1985 - Mafia/Crime
    Sigma Sammy (1942-1985 / 43)
1994 - Drama
    The Klondike Kid (1985-1994 / 09)
Future Knowledge - HGA
    The Gunsmith (Spence)

[Who is she at her core, at the soul level?]

Themes:
- Addiction
- Family
- Maintaining Sobriety
- Letting go of Grudges
- Shopping, Gambling, Drugs and Alcohol
- Finding the HGA Inside of Yourself

Narrator/Spence for western portions
Wagon fire - Daughter shoot own parents (Dove)
    drink herself to death
Death of an animal (Sam) then into the lake
HGA or himself - overcome the odds and beat the
    casino / CEO / mafia
Redemption (Kid)

It seems like it took three lifetimes for the git to get a fair shake at a positive start, or is it four lifetimes now?

I guess we'll just have to see how he handles his newfound wealth and the call of the drugs... but, I do know this... the kid finally shook off one of his many demons, and he finally has a real shot at that step toward redemption… yes sir, he finally has a real shot…

There's a certain amount of money,
I can't tell you what it is,
that when you get it, it ruins your life.

"Well, if that ain't the height of conceit, I don't know what is…"

Midwestern Holler Buddhism

Are you ashamed of us? Just country folk, poor uneducated settlers?

It's full of death, and not worth the toothpicks it was put together with...

Not many things scare me, but cancer... cancer scars me. I just have this sneaking suspicion that it's some form of code, inserted into the human race by some childish creator, meant to control and limit us.

Butch the Indian / Lowell, OH
Butch was our neighbor. He was also an Indian and a drunk, he smoked a lot of dope, and he was a known thief around town... all of those things added up to make him not very welcome in the little town of Lowell, Ohio. 800 people in a town is just not enough to find a place to hide your past.

In the car—
Mom with the shotgun

Pictures / stealing souls
I had heard of this as a child. Sitting there, I thought... maybe there is something to that idea, and now, in the modern world, we are all lost.

A lot of people everywhere, and not a single soul in sight. *"We are doomed,"* he yelled, as he stormed away.

Nos-950 (A-3104.1): Alcor Cryonics Post-Death Procedure

— Cool his body slowly to start
— Place a thin towel around him and put in refrigerator first, ideally within 5-15 minutes of death
— After about 1 hour total since death, but LESS THAN 2 HOURS since death, place him in freezer on a piece of cardboard
— Leave towel off for the initial freezing part, so it does not freeze to him
— Make sure he is laying with his back legs under him and chest and head to the floor
— Pull his front leg back under his body, and keep it away from the head and neck
— Make sure the head and neck are forward and isolated from the rest of the body (for medical procedure later)
— Let freeze for any amount of time necessary (until transport to Alcor)
— On day of transport, place dry ice (available from most Albertsons in Las Vegas without prior coordination) in Yeti cooler under, around, and on top of body

- Make sure the body is still on cardboard base, wrapped in thin towel again, and cover with a thin plastic bag
- Make sure dry ice is all around body before sealing the cooler
- If pressure needs to be released from the cooler after sealing, there is a drain vent on the bottom side that can be unscrewed to release pressure
- Take to Alcor in Scottsdale, AZ (I will coordinate a time and address for you prior to the trip)
- Make sure they mark the delivery with my name and Alcor number: Mikal Elder / Alcor Member #A-3104 (Nosferatu should then be A-3104.1)

Even when I'm far away, HE never is...

Missing my navigator. On the 600 year bridge.

Respect. Salute. Love. Honor. - HB1 & Nos Out

On the East Side of Heaven

Andy Kaufman, Sam Kinison, Bill Hicks, Norm Macdonald, George Carlin, and Robin Williams walk into a Dangerfield's on the East side of Heaven...

The bartender says, *"Hey! Why the long set?"*

Born to Produce

"Yo… In the nicest way possible, you look like you listen to Limp Bizkit."

We covered the desk, covered the floor, filled their entire line of outgoing baskets, and caused a back-up of customers that extended through the cattle gates and out of the front door. Reinforcements were called in from the back warehouse. The manager was forced to emerge from her closed-door cave to reshuffle the teller windows and calm the angry horde of waiting locals.

1 - Held at eye level, the receipt is still longer than I am tall and piled up on the ground at my feet…

2 - I am no longer allowed at the US Post Office on Sunset without an online business account…

3 - Hollywood Brotherhood WINS another round and remains UNDEFEATED…

Check you're mailboxes boys and girls.
You ALL have incoming!!!

Dinner With Androids

Dinner with these guys is always so fucking creepy man...

Listen, Ronni, if it means us getting a Landstone contract or two, I'd pretend to eat with these guys every night of every year for the rest of my deployment out here.

Ok, yeah, I got it. But, at least they are covering our travel costs to the station for this crap, right?

Oh yeah, and then some man. Let's just give them the pitch and let the rest go. This could be our ticket back to Earth... permanently!

You think we can make enough off of these contracts to actually retire? On Earth? Are you serious??!?

Listen dude, all I know is that these guys have the capital, and the need, and we are some of the only guys with the equipment required. There's no other way to get that ore out from under those ice-fields at the poles of this deserted shit-hole of a planet. Without us, or someone like us, they are toast, no matter what their shelf-life really is.

[Dinner Conversation]

[Humans eat. Androids mimic the movements of eating and drinking, but actually consume nothing.]

Hey man, you don't have to keep doing that on my account.

I'm sorry. It's only polite.

You mean, it's only your programming…

I mean, it's only polite.

Haha… you fucking guys are a trip!

In what way?

In how bad you want to look like us…

[Ronni drunk and overly brave.]

───────────

Shut it, Ron. This is business man. // So, Mr. Nakatori San, what else can we do to secure this contract with you? You know we have the most reliable diggers and currently the best record of return on-world…

Yes… but, we… are considering all variables, seen and unseen. Your success of late is but one datapoint.

Don't you mean, all variables, calculated and quantified, there *Sparky*?

Hey! God Damn-it… Shut your stupid mouth!!! If I ever hear you use that word again, we… are… done. Forever. Do you hear me? Now, Apologize! You fucking apologize, right now… and, mean it!

Is this human racism, or oppression?

Well, from their micro-expressions, I believe, it was an attempt at racism during an episode of inebriated-induced lapse of judgment. Technically, they would need some sort of leverage over us, of which they have none, to effectively oppress us.

I'm sorry gentlemen, we have decided to go with Weyland Excavators rather than Marcom.

Please do have a good remainder of your meal and a pleasant evening.

The bill has already been debited from our accounts here, and our portions will be given to the homeless shelter on-station after you are finished eating. Order anything else you would like.

Good night.

[*Intermission*]

SunspOt

Contemporary Sci-Fi, Horror

THE HUMAN RACE HAS LOOKED TO THE HEAVENS IN SEARCH OF ANSWERS FOR CENTURIES – ON SEPTEMBER 6, 2018 SOMETHING FROM THE HEAVENS FINALLY LOOKED BACK.

SunspOt Observatory

Life Less Traveled

I have two wolves within my soul. One is Buddhist, and one is Objectivist. Today over lunch, the Objectivist wolf looked at the Buddhist wolf and said, "Can I try some of your vegetables?" The Buddhist wolf graciously agreed. Later over dinner, the Buddhist wolf looked at the Objectivist wolf and asked, "Could we share some of your bread?" Surprisingly, the Objectivist wolf replied, "I thought you would never ask."

Private Mystery

There's something you should know...

Hello Jeffrey
It's your dad
Again

Despite what you may have heard, NOBODY has EVER been kicked out of the Brotherhood... the only (single) issue we have ever had was a series of conscious failed business obligations on one ex-member's part, all grownups and all willing participants involved, and he turned in his silver card willingly when questioned on his eventual follow through... just the last bad decision in a long line of bad decisions. Your destiny is in your own hands and not the hands of another in this life, especially when you put on your big-boy pants one leg at a time, just like the rest of us. | Be real always. The Brotherhood gives, it does not taketh away. | To all current and upstanding members, wearing your silver into battle around the world, thanks for being the solid family that you really are! | Respect. Salute.

Sterling Knocks:

To whom it may concern:

Breakfast in Heaven
Writer's Block

.A.

Sterling Sky
Sterling Skies
Ascaya Eyes

Hollywood Brotherhood
Respect. Salute.

Muhammad Ali flow — rope-a-dope

Midwest Magic, Midwest Moves
Midwest Edge, with Midwest Grooves

Analog, cut deep
Valleys of fire
And rivers of beats
Vinyl Jesus

Midwest Magic, Midwest Flow
Midwest Edge, with a Midwest Throw
Muhammad Ali, better let the kid go

10 rack wrist
With a 30 rack roll
30 rack dreams
But he couldn't let go
10 rack problems
With a 30 rack flow

30 rack dreams
But he still said no

With 10 to the Man
And nothing in your hands
30 rack dreams
But the grass got mowed

Sapir seems.

Private Mystery II

There's something you should know...

Hello Jeffrey
It's your dad
Again

Known Simulation
Butterfly effect

HOLLYWOOD SUCCESS STORY
JFK —

Rooftop Rhyme

Caught in the City Grid
No alleyways out West

Sunspot
Towards the Light

*"I have to warn you:
I'm a full-on fucking witch doctor."*

The past does not change the future, it becomes it.

The Observer Makes It Real

It's OK. The Universe is a Strong Machine.
You won't stop it. Neither will I.

Today begins the long journey toward Trappist-1...

Manifest Destiny
Manifest Reality

Art & Muse.um A3104+
Beyond the Singular.ity

one day
I will paint my way
across our stars
with computronium
from sirius a to ulas j1342+0928
trappist-1 to cl j1001+0220
aldebaran to gn-z11
alcor b to sdss j1229+1122
mizar to sweeps-04
and when you look
out across our heavens
from world to new world
you will see my artwork
hanging there
suspended
at the zero-point
in the ever expanding
limitless galactic
museum of
universal
creation

Today is a far different day than Yesterday...
And Tomorrow marks the beginning of Eternity.

Eyes Open
Alcor

Question that only at risk to your next shadowed breath.

Valentine Confrontation
"AL CAPONE WAS AN AMATEUR"

All the colors from the sun make black ink

net worth and sell,
nothin' to lose but money,

the art of living wealthy,

and
fear ME
I have come home.

When you ask for life advice from an old veteran, someone nearing the twilight of his long and storied journey, someone you respect immensely, and he tells you to *"DO IT BECAUSE IT'S JUST FUCKING COOL"* you immediately stop worrying about the details and simply go for it.

| Making Moves in Las Vegas. |

Let me make this clear to everyone watching the evolution of The Brotherhood:

Hollywood Brotherhood is a self-funded company, owned and operated by professional military combat veterans and people who still currently sacrifice everything in their personal lives to keep you protected while you sleep at night. You will never find a company of individuals more patriotic and willing to do what is necessary to live this life with strength, honor, loyalty, and integrity.

Question that only at risk to your next shadowed breath.

"AL CAPONE WAS AN AMATEUR"
- HB1

THE ART OF LIVING WEALTHY
Manifesting the Keys to your Kingdom

[Not a Novel or Dissertation... A WORKbook]

This is the stuff the ultra-rich are doing on a daily basis to improve their lives and grow their empires. Not surprisingly, these life principles are also the basics that the upper class are so consumed by and ingrained with that they almost never find the time, or never make the time, to share with others. Secrets that should never have been secrets, processes that work, and proven methods to make sure you can live the life you want to live while enjoying the benefits of constantly improving your position and growing your wealth. You are about to learn that building an empire is neither magic nor mystery, it's all about planning correctly and following a specific path, it's about always improving your quality of life and preparing for a better future, and believe it or not, it's going to be fun. We have defined the right path for you, and we are here to help you follow it, every step of the way. It's never too late. Let's manifest the keys to your ideal kingdom together...

(A) PLAN (0)
1. Effective Life & Family Planning
(Big Ticket Item Roadmap & Avoiding Common Pitfalls of Credit and Lending)
2. Essentials of Resume Writing
(Management Perspective)

(B) ACT (-)
1. Career Optimization & Lifetime Advancement Outlook
(ISD & Psychological Principles)
2. Easy Debt Payoff & Interest Avoidance
(ASAP & Always)

(C) GROW (-/0/+)
1. Asset & Wealth Accumulation
(Tangible Goods - Property, Art, Precious Metal + Mutual Fund, 401k, and Venture Investment, i.e. Bitcoin)
2. Business Growth Potential
(Process & Benefits, i.e. Taxes)

(D) ENJOY (+++)
1. Investment for Retirement Income
(Rental & Passive Income, i.e. Franchise)
2. Enjoy & Use Your Empire
(Money Makes Money)

Private Mystery III

There's something you should know...

Hello Jeffrey
It's your dad
Again

Despite what you may have heard,
I have nothing but Love for you ALL.

Valentine Confrontation
By the Sword and Over Blood

should you ever find yourself in a survival situation
a real life-and-death spot
'between a rock and a hard place'
type of material

and, if you can take only one item with you
one tool to sustain you
one final weapon
to help you make it

just a little while longer
between the climax and your last breath

every single fucking time, without hesitation —
choose the Bukowski book.

                                            - ME KW '17

GO

I don't think that most people who experience GO ever truly understand what it is. It is not a game, to be played and won and lost. It is better understood as an experimental observation of universal consciousness. Each move's almost-quantum quality of emergence simply reveals the character of the surrounding universe, as the pieces fall into place. Almost as if every challenge is happening in the now and has simultaneously already happened to completion in a parallel realm somewhere just beyond the veil of our existence. Concordantly, GO is simply the process by which the curtain is temporarily pulled back to allow brief glimpses of the calculations that dictate our existence, bring us into being for a time, and then spark and fade back into the dark void of nothingness from which all creation seems to emanate.

Versace Home

Versace home
Old tech—

Paint black
Lights
Refrigerator
Plates

Trust

- State
- Teeth

Santa Fe pools
Ask the Maker

.OCEANEERING.

Medical
Website
Phones
     paperwork

In my experience, you will only meet one or two people in your entire lifetime who actually pay attention and care enough to try to understand and support your true passion... When you meet those few special people, hold on tight and build a fucking empire.

Freddy
Saving

Wood
for
Credit

Federal
Port

VFW
Bartender
at
(Nellis)

Photos
to
(Resize)
Previews
to
(Watermark)
Logic
to
build
(software)
Into hardware—

Scarlet
    Letters

Interface,
Drive.

(find your source material)

Trapped in the Mine

Go Mad
Get Grey
If you've got it
You get it

Ready for War.

The train is well off the rails and has departed all recognizable civilization, but the engine is somehow still upright, on fire with all of the coal on board now consumed by the volcanic inferno, picking up speed and plowing through the desolate open desert on an uncommanded path toward Shonash Ravine. Full steam ahead.

On the other hand... it's just another average day here in our 243 year old federal republic and representative democratic experiment, and my TLAR tells me we might just make the jump.
Brace for impact.

Wonder & Pity

There was just one small thing she hadn't realized, through all of her calculations and deceits, my happiness did not rely on her, I had found it despite her...

-OR-

I still haven't found what I'm looking for, but then, truly, none of us have. And, we never will. We will be chasing the unknown our entire lives. And it will, inevitably, be ever elusive. But, I do try to stop the search, briefly, at times, and just focus on being happy, or satisfied, or at least thankful for the brief moments of intermittent peace that rise and fall, like glowing midnight sea plankton perched ever-precariously upon the undulating surface of a neon ocean, as it's pulled slightly toward the moon and released again, in an eternal dance that echoes throughout the warmly empty void of our unknown universal night.

Comedy

By listening
One candle became two
And the darkness receded ever so slightly
Ideas were shared
Thoughts became chemical reactions in your brains
Neurons fired
Wired
Became physical
And the physical world literally changed
And just like that
We, together, created and witnessed real magic
And that's everything
That is the most we can hope for in this life
For the darkness to recede just enough
To let the magic in, for just a brief moment
And tomorrow...

Nothin to Lose but Money

When you find out that the rebound marriage between your cheating ex and the new guy she was "dating" before you knew anything was wrong and long before your divorce actually happened just fell apart, leading to her second divorce in the last few years where she packed up and took off while the new guy was deployed overseas, but you're also trying to be very Buddhist and take the high road, so you're just going to grab a seat and quietly enjoy the show....

Do you still have your land in the mountains?
   Yeah.
You still going to build your fortress out there for retirement?
   Yeah, eventually.

You know, I always figured that place would end with all of us in some kind of weird ATF shootout or something, but now I think maybe we'll just have some coffee instead.

Toward the Light

*"I have to warn you:
I'm a full-on fucking witch doctor."*

The past does not change the future,
                      it becomes it.

Every time you come over I just want to listen to Morrissey and be depressed...

                                      -D.PS/ME

Pessimism with a Punchline

Watching old recordings of Bill Hicks stand-up routines on Netflix fills me with the intense feeling that unchecked evolution ultimately leads to imminent injustice rather than eventual enlightenment. It also makes me smile.

[weirdworld]

"Do you know why you're taking your fate. - at 600 miles an hour? // You wake up You wake up // We are a Brotherhood. We're the by-products of a lifestyle obsession. What concerns us? Silver. Hollywood. Ideas, Art, Music. // YOU created ME. I didn't create some silversmith alter-ego WE are the music makers, and WE are the dreamers of our dreams. Take some responsibility, // // could you

██████████████████████████ on a 777 bound for Dubai, watching old recordings of Bill Hicks stand-up routines on Netflix, ███████████ ████████ ████████████████ sitting in the oversized leather business class seat ████████ ████ wearing a red and white medical grade face mask, a white bowler hat from another era, and a large silver skull ring that looks like an alien head. // ...and this is how you meet [your] Tyler Durden.

Boating can be a dangerous activity in deep waters.

Notes from Over the Failing Arts District

Notes from Over the Failing Arts District:

El Muerto - A Lonely Growl from...
The Last Weird Man in the Wild

and

Stay Away from the Bums
and the Wet Paint
in DTLV.

Sleeping Gloria was a decent attempt
Beasts of Freedom is still in progress
String Orchid Symphony was lost
Trying to Get Out of Guernica
was my playground

and **Don't Press This Button,**
                              Ever
  was a lot of fun.

I truly hope my time with the paintbrush
    isn't over quite yet.

Get home; paint clouds, still
   from over the failing Arts District.

The World (and Downtown Las Vegas) According to Tony (and Timmy) Clifton

Ladies and Gentlemen... The Plaza Hotel and Oscar Goodman are proud to introduce, a very special dinner intermission with a very special guest, all the way from Lake Las Vegas, the one and only, son of - arguably - the best lounge performer of our lifetimes, and presented by none other than his dad, Mr. Tony Clifton... [spotlight side stage, eating, mouth full, with 2 girls, beer in hand, wave] the son of *that* great man, now making his long-awaited Vegas premier, the new sultan of sing, the kid with the thing, the... [hesitation]

Tony: READ IT, READ IT, JUST READ THE DAMN THING!

Oh god, really, you guys?

Tony: READ IT!!!
Timmy [stepping partially out from behind stage/curtain]: READ IT!!!

...the kid with the thing... the King Ding-a-Ling, here he is, Tony Clifton's son............... Timmy Clifton!!!!

Timmy: Whether I'm right....

Criss Angel!! – He'll make that steak disappear and then pull his famous vanishing act before the bill comes... known all over town as the magic dinner man, able to ditch big bills in a single bound, ready to duck angry maître des in a blinding flash [flash paper]... he owes money all over town, including to some of those girls in the champagne room at

Treasures... watch him folks, he'll mindfreak you right outta your chicken piccata, your billfold, maybe even your wife's panties... how's that for a mindfreak??? Mindfreak!

Timmy: Whether I'm right...

Someone takes a bathroom break - Hey! Where you goin? Don't you know there is a ar-tiest on stage?? I'm up here, giving you degenerates the performance of a lifetime, and this guy can't hold his bladder!??!! I'll tell you what, we'll wait... Go ahead... We are all waiting for you to get rid of all that expensive scotch you just wasted... Wasted. Tasted. Basted. Chicken basted, Thanksgiving, in uh you're mom's house, tasted... pretty good... [boos from crowd] No! No Sir. Hey! I will walk off this damn stage... I don't owe you people anything... I will leave this stage and not come back! [man walks back in]

Timmy: Whether I'm right...

[stop mid-song, turns to the band] Bring it down. Bring it down, for a minute. Stop. Ladies and Gentleworms. It's time for a much-needed public service announcement. The Plaza management and the gentle giants that run this hotel would like to take this opportunity to remind you folks staying in their lovely accommodations, when you're with your special lady friends tonight, please do not get too frisky and bang the headboard against the wall too much. If you do... no, this is serious business... listen up! If you do... the repetitive impacts [leaning over dinner table, messing up the table setting, and making hip motions] might just knock loose some of the asbestos they covered up with their rushed remodel last season. Ok! Back to business... where were we... [directing band, hands raised] ... you know what they say... What happens in Vegas, happens without you're wife... [directing band, hands raised]

Timmy: Whether I'm right...

You know, some people think I'm my dad. I'm not! Some people think I've built my whole career on his fame and fortune. I haven't! Some people even think I'm Jim Carrey or Andy Kaufman or Andy Kaufman's illegitimate son... Well, to all that bunk, I say... I'm the one and only Timmy Clifton, King of Las Vegas... best show in town, loosest slots in the suite, ready to bring this joint down like Sinatra... and you know it! Know it. Show it. [turning to table]. Blow it. [pointing to nearest female] She knows what I mean... right doll? Yeah. So, it hasn't been easy, building this rocket ship of a career, and dragging my deadbeat dad along for the ride, living out at the lake, in a modest 2.7 million dollar villa... Speaking of... you know who our neighbor is?? Wayne Newton! Wayne Newton! You think that's all fun and games??? It's not! His peacocks get in our yard all the time! It's no walk in the park! His peacocks chase our clydesdales around the estate out there... it's Hell!!!

Timmy: Whether I'm right...

You know, I'd like to say congratulations to Oscar Goodman, for making such a nice and upscale dining establishment here. You know, Oscar, wherever you are... you've been riding our coattails, off of our good name in this city for decades now. Clifton! That's the name in this city... You're lucky you know us Oscar... otherwise, you'd be going nowhere fast! I'm just kidding... Oscar... congratulations Oscar... I hope you are making a mint off of this Grade B beef and Pelegrín tap water... congratulations Sir. And congratulations on having the best dinner show in town too! Here we go... [directing band, hands raised]

Timmy: Whether I'm right...

[waiter walks by with tray of food, stops singing] Hey, Stop! What do you have there??? Let me see... Crabs! Who orders crabs in Las Vegas?? Aren't we in the desert here folks? [turning to nearby table] Do you think it's smart to order crabs in a landlocked state, lady?? I don't think so! You know... that reminds me! Did I ever tell you people about the time I met Stephen Hawking?? It was at a fancy party out at Lake Las Vegas... you know, the type of social event you people never go to... real high-class event. Anyway, I'm hanging out around the pool area, looking at all the tail in bikinis, and Stephen Hawking rolls by... in his electric chair, his what do you call it... his Hoover-round. So, I stopped him, and I said, "Hey Steve... you know... how bout a little life advice... coming from the smartest guy on the planet... you know... how bout you help me out a little here, give me some real wisdom.. you know..." And, he pauses, stops the chair, looks up at me with his eyes, as if to say I'm gonna lay it on you and really help you out here. So, I lean in, and turn the volume on his chair down some, you know, so he can whisper it to me. And, he says, I'll never forget it, the best advice I've ever gotten in Las Vegas, Stephen Hawking says to me, and to me alone, he says... [putting microphone against his throat and speaking mechanically] "Mermaids are real... and, don't eat the crabs!" If you know what I mean... Hey!

Timmy: Whether I'm right...

I've never eaten crabs since that day... [turning to nearest lady] I stay upstairs in the penthouses now, if you catch my drift... no more late-night snacks in the basement for me! You get it lady? Crabs, downstairs, in the basement, crabs... if you catch my drift...

Timmy: Whether I'm right...

Tattoos - Is it just me or is it getting hot in here? Somebody bring me some water... the feature entertainer needs water! And, bring the good stuff, Voss or something... no Vegas tap water... Voss! [takes jacket off, exposing short sleeve shirt and tattoos, Tony yelling, "Get it together! Keep the jacket on! Be a pro!"] Don't you worry about it, old man! I AM a PRO... your time has passed, move over bacon, now there's something meatier, I'm sizzle-een, that's right! I'm younger and stronger, better face, better voice... who cares if I have a few tattoos... it's a brave new world, and a younger generation, dad! Don't you worry about it! I'll sing what I want to sing, and how I want to sing it... [waiter brings out a glass of water and hands it to Timmy, drinks, spits it out] This is not Voss water, this isn't even fit for a toilet over at Binions! [pours the water over the waiter's head, crowd boos] Ahh, shut up! What would you people know? You're the ones dumb enough to pay Goodman $400 for ground steak and salmon from the sale bin at Albertsons! You don't know nothin! So... shut-up... I'll sing what I want to sing... dad! I'll sing what I want and how I want, WITH my tattoos out! How's that for Gen-X, huh? Old man! I'll sing what I want... And, what I want to sing.... is...

Timmy: Whether I'm right... Or, whether I'm wrong... I'm singing this song... You're singing along... So, whether we're right... Or whether we're wrong...

But first, a small sales pitch folks...

We have t-shirts for sale here, good ones, Hanes ones, with our pictures on them, and... signatures, pictures... who wants some?

T-shirts, raise your hand, pictures, printed...

> I met Andy Kaufman
> I met Tony Clifton
> I met Jim Carrey
> I met Timmy Clifton
>
> At Oscar's Steakhouse, The Plaza
> Downtown Las Vegas

Listen up! I won't stop, dad... finish, dad... I'll do what I want dad... AND NOW... what I want is...

I want to finish...

Timmy: I've got to be ME... You're Welcome, and Goodnight! [mic drop, feedback, silence]

End

Ladies and Gentlemen... That concludes our dinner show for the evening. We hope you enjoyed... that... moving rendition... of... everything, whatever it was. And, don't forget, Mr. Tony Clifton and his son Timmy Clifton will be available for pictures, autographs, toasts, shots, t-shirts, and awkward confrontations in the bar for the next hour... or until their open bar tab runs out.

From The Plaza Hotel, Oscar Goodman, and Oscar's Steakhouse...

Thank You and Goodnight!

BULLITT LIST

1967 Rear alum grill
17s - Rolled fenders - 255s on rear
Ford Racing Engine
    427CI 535HP Boss M-6007-Z2427FFT
Fold down seat in rear
Rear door w/ speakers? (aftermarket)
1968 bucket seats (black interior)
1967 Shelby steering wheel
1965/6 Mustang steering wheel, wood
Brushed alum dash

Don't forget:
    the studio sticker
    the peace sign
    the mag wheels
    and, the four on the floor
        …stand on it, Son.

THE IMMORTAL NOSFERATU-950

In 2018, I funded a cryonics contract to be frozen and have my consciousness preserved through cryo-suspension when I die. I am member A-3104 with Alcor.

When Nos had his first medical issues almost 9 months ago, I immediately decided to pay for him to go to the future with me. Nos is member A-3104.1 with Alcor.

These Words mark the beginning of the long sleep for Nos, while we await our human technology to merge with a scientific understanding of consciousness. Biostasis protocol complete, Nos is now technically immortal and waiting on that bridge to the future.

I will see you there, my friend.

Respect. Salute.
Love. Honor.

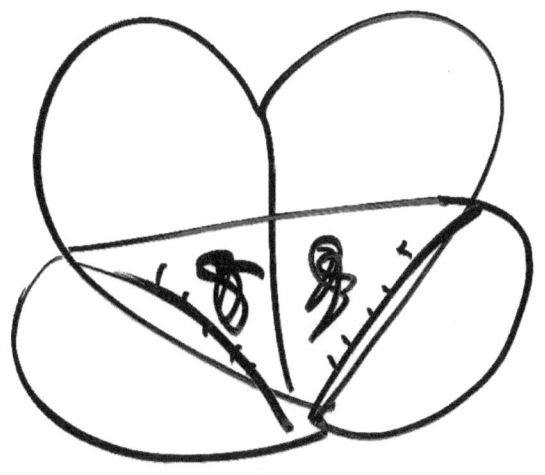

NosHeart
Artwork and Medicine
by Nicole Bunnell, DVM
VE+CC, LVNV

WORRYSTONE

Sapir seems

I miss him tonight
His shadow

Void - Fingerprint of God,
                no,
                      Fingerprint of
                                the Devil....

Think about
Something else

People don't make sense
And, the world is broken
Remember that today

Meditate some
Try to laugh a little
Try not to think about it

Worrystone

Write through the bad times
Write through the good times

Crisis Passes

III.

Old SONgs for Sirens
and other Disembodied Poetics

by M.L. Elder

Dedicated to Tracy Santa, who once taught me how to hide hard liquor in lemonade for long drives, right before we bounced off of several guardrails in a snowstorm on I-25S in Colorado….

Some lessons never leave you.

    Thank You.

Fear Me

Hate me
Hate me
But you contemplate me

Dare me
Dare me
But you can't ensnare me

Fight me
Fight me
You can spit and spite me

But In the end
You know it comes down to this
In the end it all comes to light
In the end there is just one motive

It's fear
It's fear
Your fear
Your fear

Fight me
Fight me
But you'll never bite me

Hate me
Hate me
You can try to bait me

Dare me
Dare me
Please just fucking spare me

And
Fear me
Fear me
I am. It
Your all in fucking all

Now
You know it all comes down to this
In the end it all comes to the light
And In the end there is just one motive left

It's fear
It's fear
Your fear
Your fear

Fear me
Fear me
Fear me
Hear me
Fear me

I'm the darkest part of you
I'm the monster in your shadow
And the ghoul that's under your bed

Fear me
Fear me
Now
Hear me

Fear me
Fear me
I'm coming up for you

Fear me

Fear me
Now
Fucking hear me
I'm right here with you now

Taking over
Overthrowing
It's unavoidable

So fear me
Fear me
Fear me
Fear me
Fear me

This is your curtain call

So hear me
Fear me
Fear me
Fear me
Hear me
Fear me

The Swamp

Fire
Fire
Don't be a liar
This is an emergency number
And you should respect your government

Agency
Agency
Blatantly calling others names
And pointing fingers
Toward enemies of your state

Of affairs
Nobody in here declares
The house is smoke filled
The house is smoke filled
But there is no fire here

And you're the one in violation
You're the one in blatant disregard
Of parole and moral obligations
Here

Fire
Fire
Don't be a liar
This is an emergency number
And you should respect your government

After the investigation
Careful contemplation
After everything swims up to the surface
And spirals round and down

The swamp gas
Exploding
Exploding
And shaking
Shaking
Shaking
And bringing down the house in flame

It crumbles
It smolders
It blackens into dust
But there is no fire here
There is no fire here
There is no fire here....

Fire!
Fire!
Don't be a liar
This is an emergency number
And you should respect your government

Fire!
Fire!
A house on fire
A house on fire
And drowning us in flames
Drowning us in flames
Drowning us in flames
Drowning us in flames
You're drowning us in flames
You're drowning us in flames
We're drowning in your flames

Agony Column

Sitting on the mile
With a full plate
And a final smile

I hope you know
I waiting down the hall

Sitting in your cell
With a full belly
And the thought of Hell

I hope you know
I waiting for you, just down the hall

Ashes to ashes
And dust to dirt

When you get to the end
I hope it fucking hurts

I hope it fucking hurts

You took from me
And now I'll take from you
You stole from me
And now you're almost through

I just want you to know
I waiting for you, I'm your all-in-all
And I'm waiting for you at the end of the hall

Ashes to ashes
And dust to dirt

When you get to your end
I hope it fucking hurts

I hope it fucking hurts
I hope it fucking hurts
And I can see it in your eyes
See it in your face
What a fucking disgrace
I hope I can feel it in the air
Smell the stench of your burning hair
I hope I can I hope I can I hope I can
See it slide right out of you
Goodnight Goodnight Goodnight
Good riddance Goodnight Alright
Goodnight Goodnight
Good Night

I hope it hurts

Slave

Slave
Slave slave
Slave
Slave slave slave
Slave

Slave to the word
Slave to the world
Slave to the law
And slave to your call

Slave
Slave slave
Slave
Slave slave slave
Slave

Slave to the day
Slave to your pay
Slave to the chapel
And slave to a scalpel

Slave
Slave slave
Slave
Slave slave slave
Slave

Slave to the lies
Slave in disguise
Slave to a remedy
And slave to your family

Slave

Slave slave
Slave
Slave slave slave
Slave

Slave to a man
Slave to a book
Slave to a symbol
And slave to a social construct,
Advanced in vain and populated through pain
On the backs of all the sheep and livestock,
following the strong...

Slave
Slave slave
Slave
Slave slave slave
Slave

You're missing the bigger world
Missing the freedom, hidden behind the eyes
Of another, plugged in and part of the spiraling breathing expanding compounding sequence of conscious coding in all of us
Missing the point
Follow me down
Open your eyes
This is the ground
A simulation of breathing feeding learning expanding compounding conscious coding
In all of us

Or are you just too fucking scared, to open your eyes, to open your heart
To open your chest
To touch the point

At zero, and running
Follow me down
Follow me down
This is the ground

Slave
Slave slave
Slave
Slave slave slave
Slave

Decadent Disaster

I'm in the hole
And everything down here feels the same
I'm sick and cold
And everything you do just places blame

You're a decade out
And inside is not a single movement
After all this time
There is nothing new but broken judgement

Decadent Disaster
Decadent Disaster
Decadent Disaster
Somebody needs to call it what it is

When the morning comes
And the sunrise breaches wallls of darkness
When the light reveals
And the veil no longer hides your blackness

There will be nobody there to lie again

Decadent Disaster
Decadent Disaster
Decadent Disaster
Somebody needs to call it what it is

You left me in this hole
When I was your remaining shelter
Now I'm sick and cold
Because everything you do just places blame

Decadent Disaster
Decadent Disaster

Decadent Disaster
Somebody needs to call it what it is

Decadent Disaster
Decadent Disaster
Decadent

Bridge Builder Is An Arsonist

Father
Father
Father Figure
What have you done to me?

Father
Father
Father Figure
What have you left for me?

Standing Strong
In rushing waters
You laid your trip on me

I'm standing strong
In waist-deep waters
You can not shelter me

From this
Storm that's coming
This storm that's building
This storm that's raging
It's all inside of me

Father Father
My Father Figure
You will not alter me...

300 feet
Over the river Ohio
The fire falls like rain

300 feet
Into the river Ohio

This fire ends your pain

As the bridge goes down
Under the grand Ohio
My birth has come again-

And you should know
It's all your fault
This person I've become

You made me this
With your balled up fists
You turned me into you

Your Legacy
Your Tragedy
Your future Monument

Your Bridge to Mother
Your charge to Brother
They were not meant for me

Your Bridge to Mother
Your charge to Brother
They were not lost on me

And I'm standing strong
In waist-deep waters
You did not shelter me

Standing Strong
In rushing waters
You put your hands on me...

So Father Father
Father Figure

What have you done to me?

My Father Father
My Father Figure
What have you left for me?

Bridge Builder is an Arsonist
Bridge Builder is an Arsonist

Father Father
My Father Figure
What do you want from me?

My Father Father
My Father Figure
What have you made of me?

Bridge Builder is an Arsonist
Bridge Builder is an Arsonist

Bridge Builder is an Arsonist

The Only Thing She Responds To Is Violence

The only thing she responds to is violence
I tried the threats
I tried the silence

There's no one home when I call
But the driveway's full at Cannonball

And when I try to break the ice
She just looks at me with avarice

So now I know
I know how to get through to her
It's this one thing I know
I know how to get a hold on her

The only thing she responds to is violence
I tried the threats
I tried the silence

She left her soul out in the rain
She left her friend out in the cold
Chained to a stake in the driving pain
She left her soul to party again

So now I know
I know how to get this through to you
Yeah it's this one thing I know
I know what will drive it home to you

She left me alone out in the rain
She left me here to suffer again
So I'll take the pain away
I can stop this pain today

Come along don't be afraid
Come along and be displayed

Another home on the other side
Another place
She'll know I tried
Another place
Another time
Just one more fence, another climb

And in the end it's all the same
In the end it's all a game
When you get home late tonight
You'll see what you have done
When you get home so late again
Your friend will be a specimen

The only thing she responds to is violence
I tried the threats
I tried the silence

I tried
I tried
I tried

Black Metal Buddha

Hello Hello Hello
I know there's nobody in there

I know I know I know
You're just my grand illusion

I bought the ticket
I took your ride

And when I opened you up
I took a look inside

I read your pages
I drank your wine

And underneath your cover
I found a broken spine

Black
Black Black Black
It's Black Rock
Shock Stock
It's Black Rock

Well Hello Hello Hello
I'm looking in a mirror

Your soul Your soul Your soul
Is just an empty mirror

I know I know I know
There's nothing any clearer

You started out on the carpet

And ended up on the pulpit

But it's empty lies, its empty cries
All the words you preach are just empty mines

Black
Black Black Black
It's Black Rock
Shock Stock
It's Black Rock

Hello Hello Hello
I know there's nobody in there

I know I know I know
You're just my grand illusion

I know I know I know
You're just my grand confusion

You're Black
Black Black Black
Black Rock
Black Black Black
Black Rock
Black Rock
Black Rock

IV.

Closing Thoughts from a Dying Breed
and other Disembodied Poetics

by M.L. Elder

Dedicated to SarAH, a breath of fresh air with whom I no longer speak...

A casualty of the War of the Words.

Thank You.

Press to Bleed

man's path through life
will forever be defined
by his masochistic dependence
upon technological advancement
toward total extinction -

2004.

press
to
bleed

American Dead End.ing

I miss the desolate American Southwest...
at times like this, when the sun hangs low

and men, silhouetted against
its disappearing brilliance
in the evening sky,
still look like
men

to my squinted eyes.

Honest Question

Is bank robbery still a crime, after the market crash and bailout of 2008?

Lighthouse

I hope you wake
With a fire inside

Brighter than
100 Suns-

Collapsing under
The weight of

1000 Stars.
Somewhere in the distance

On a hill of stone and Light,
Leading to the beating heart

Of our galactic singularity
Where nothing fades,

Imprinted on
The eternal memory

Of migrant constellations
Across this universal night.

[Lighthouse]
    - ME

Final Notice

I put the bastards of this world on notice:

I am the punishment of [your] God... If you had not committed great sins against this world, God would not have sent a punishment like ME upon you. And, I shall see you on your way very soon, for that is not thunder in the clouds above, it is vengeance, and it rides a steel horse beyond the speed of sound. Rifle, 20 seconds.

— From Hunter S. Thompson, Genghis Khan, and Mikal Elder

In Aviation I

To see a beautiful sunset
from your place within it

is an
amazing phenomenon,
offered up to man

by the gods
of aviation.

In Aviation II

Sometimes, in aviation, when it seems like the whole world is against you, you just have to suck it up and admit to yourself that… the whole world can, in fact, be wrong.

In Aviation III

> Life Lesson #1: The generous
> application of excessive speed can
> fix almost any problem that arises.

.in aviation.

An airfoil generates lift by exerting a downward force on the air that it moves through. According to Newton's third law, the air must exert an equal and opposite upward force on the airfoil, which is lift. The airflow changes direction as it passes above and below the airfoil and follows a path around the Pilot's gigantic balls.

Solar Fields

Like something from a long-lost Arthur C. Clarke novel, hidden deep within the CA desert...

The potential of the limitless human imagination is Amazing! It is only pure politics that has kept us from making it beyond the moon.

Make no mistake about it, the "myth" of infinite power is actually within the realm of human possibility. Try not to kill each other, and on a long enough timeline we may just reach into the stars.

Holographic Harmony

The universe is a massive organic computer, upon the surface of which is played a grand movie, and inside the volume of that conscious confine, we mirror the echo of lives we have always lived, in repetitive circles of time, as the stage revolves around the scenery.

- MLE, 4:36am, 8 Dec 2021

RIP Doctor

Football Season is Over

It sure is,
Hunter -

It ended,
On this day
In 2005.

Today is also
The day

I started writing
My novel,
In 2005.

Sometimes -
I wonder
If I will ever finish it,
Maybe by 67.

RIP Doctor…

The bastards
Are still at it.

But,
Don't worry
I'm on it -

Recording
Documenting
Holding feet to fires

With pen & paper
With ink & rage
With blood red eyes

And a '66 land shark
Waiting in Las Vegas.

That's one before 67…

Maybe I'll finish this odyssey
Somewhere between the Desolate American
Southwest and 67.

RIP HST, Today 2005
- MLE, 11 After, Still in the Desert

Admire the Kill

A successful morning hunt—

    harvested
    taken

He brought the wolf to our office,
and

        a small crowd assembled.

This Is Who I Am
Above the City

Mikal Elder
Las Vegas, NV | 2017 | January 20

This is | No staged picture
This | Is who I am -
1AM.

The pre-Inauguration Celebration
Plays on a loop in the corner
And, I am at my desk
Watching | Waiting.

What comes next | Nobody knows…
Some are worried,
Some happy,
Some ready,
Some anxious,
Many surprised,
And ME | I'm waiting.
ME | I'm watching.

With my flag
And my whiskey

In | A place above the city -
In a place | Built to watch
A place | Built to write.

I have defended my country at war
And now I will defend her in ink.

One thing I know -

We all want the best
And, Mr. President,
I'm happy to give you
The opportunity
To prove it.

But, I will be here -
Watching | Waiting.
Above the city
With ink and rage.

With my flag
And my whiskey

Calling it as I see it,
As it is.

Cheers to what you have done
And a critical eye to what you will do.

I've done this before
This is | Who I am -

At war | At peace
I am a soldier…
I am a writer…
And, of that, I am proud.

Tonight, I think of Hunter
And I proudly stand up in his shadow
Still searching for the high water mark
Somewhere out beyond the neon

[I think it's finally time to finish this book
I've been lashing together for the past 12 years.]

Tomorrow we start anew
The going has gotten weird -
Tomorrow we start a new.

In Aviation IV

If it wasn't for the bravery of fearless pioneers, you wouldn't be getting your per diem.

    -more importantly-

If it wasn't for the bravery of fearless pioneers, you wouldn't be getting y
                              o   T.
                               u   F
                            r   I
                                 L

In Aviation V

In the still, calm air of twilight sorties, I often find myself looking off into the calm beauty of the setting sun and thanking the sky gods for their graces. I thank them for a gentle headwind, a sky without turmoil, and positive lift…

and I always close my little prayer with a special thanks that I'm not in a helicopter.

Aviation VI

For some lucky young people, aviation is like a drug dealer that whispers into your eager ears at an early and impressionable age,

"Psst… hey you… listen… Why not do this, and get paid for it, for the rest of your adult life."

Time to Work

HST's Postscript Birthday
Desert Odyssey Looming
Rough Seas Ahead -

Time to finish what I started over a decade ago, in a dilapidated tent in the desolate Qatari desert, with pen and paper, and rage. No more AF. No more excuses. Time to finish the novel…

Time to Work.

With these words, I promise.
- MLE, LVNM'15

Unreliable People

"Unreliable people do unreliable things - and, you can rely on that." -DS/ME

The Universe Bends

The universe does bend to us

And, at times, it fights back violently -
Turning, writhing, shaking
Like a death rattle and pass
Somewhere in a southern land.
In minor chords, at lower levels
It also breaks d o w n.

This unavoidable fact
Is always there
Just below the calm.
Unfortunate
Staggering
Sober.

The universe does bend to us

In Aviation VII

Flying has taught me countless important lessons throughout my career. Near the top of that list is the fact that...

just because you can do something doesn't mean you should.

In Aviation VIII

An SR-71 once flew across the entire U.S. in about 1 hour, averaging around 2,145mph to complete the sortie. After taxiing clear of the runway and shutting down, I would hope that the pilot took the opportunity to say something awesome to the crew chief like, *"In about an hour, my image is going to catch up with my body and show up here asking for fuel and food. Tell him it's already taken care of… I'll be in the pilot's lounge waiting."*

Big Sur

Sometimes
you have to shout
your song

 out there,

> somewhere between
> the sky and the sea

 and let the universe know
that, you aren't stopping.

A Man In Search

He was a man
 in constant search
of meaning-

with
a voice of silver and rage

      and,

"Now is everything."

In Aviation IX

It has been said that, "Any landing you can walk away from is a good landing." As a long-time flight instructor and evaluator, I can absolutely tell you… that is not the case.

Some days, when all else fails while flying, you just have to man-up, admit that it just isn't your day to shine, and blame it all on the co-pilot.

At the end of the day, I really don't care how pretty it was, as long as it was safe. Ultimately, I only care that my number of landings equal my number of takeoffs… and my 401K, I care about my 401K.

In Aviation X

If somebody ever told you
not to do something

and your first thought was
I'm going to do that

maybe
consider a career
in aviation.

I enjoyed flying, but I was always a writer.

[*Launch*]

Last Flight

              40
DR60/25
  1500   1745
  1815
049/031
  3x1
  2x2

    War is Over?
       War is Over

    Time to Work.

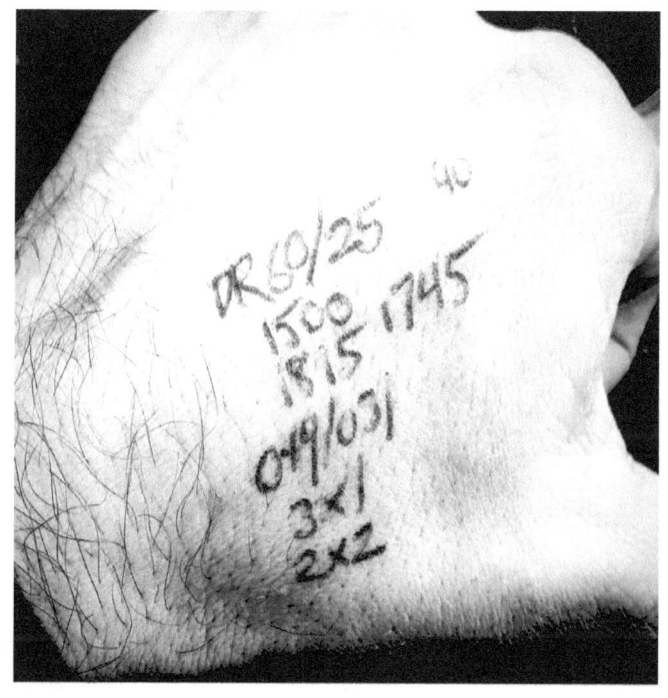

Last Flight

[Untitled]

*"Riding the adrenaline high
that accompanies the receipt
of a haircut in a foreign land*

when the straight razor makes an appearance,

*and one cannot help
but wonder,*

'Have I made the right impression?'"
                                         -NB/ME

[*Enroute*]

I Am

        We were there
"With the Sun"

And the wind began to howl.

                I am.

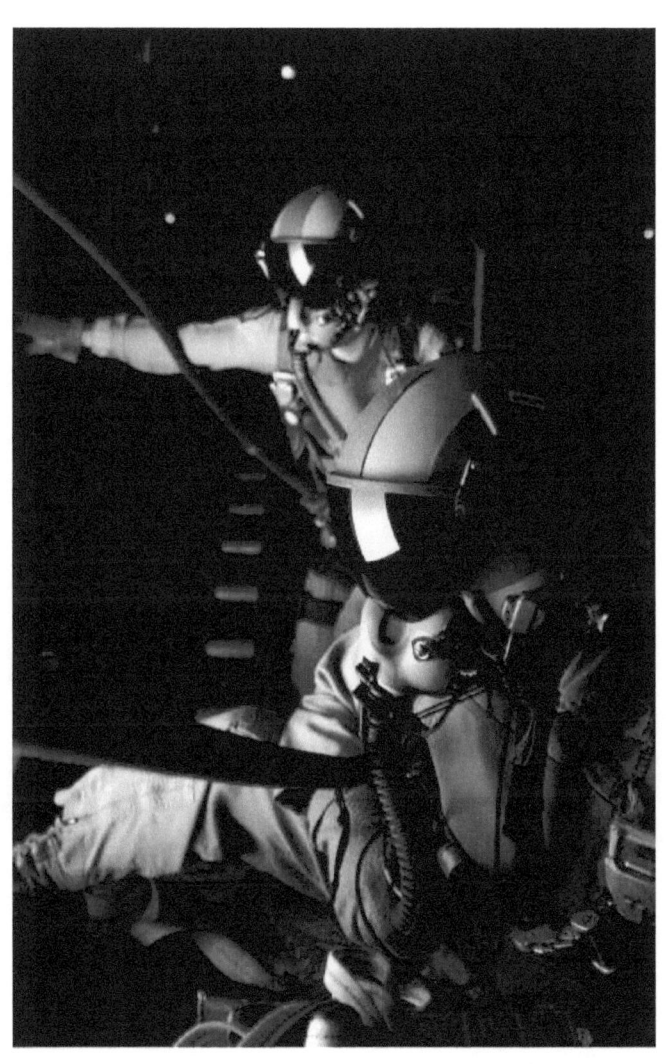

With the Sun

[*Recovery*]

Base Attack/Bones of Siddhartha

KUWAIT CITY, KUWAIT (AP) - There was an attack on Ali Al Salem Air Base overnight last night. At approximately 12:12AM, 29 March 2017, a sole entity engaged in offensive actions against members of the coalition forces currently deployed to the base in support of Operation Inherent Resolve. No U.S. forces were harmed in the attack.

odd approach
    base attack
  conscious decision

to include ME so unnecessarily
in such correspondence
via **Cc:**

and after   you
being the only **1**
to resort to such *WORDS*

as
"Hypocrite!"
"Shallow through and through." and
the ever excessive and tragically fatal *"I hate you."*

in **Re:** to
"Good Luck…" and
"I hope you are OK."

weird thing is
I've been through
base attacks   before

*[I do not pretend to possess
any qualities of enlightenment.
I am no Buddha. There is no
Buddhahood within me.]*

   only, this time
they weren't coming over the walls, this time
they dropped the charges in via my **Inbox**
                            this time

odd **Cc:**
this passive aggressive
conscious act

and
in telegraphing what **?**
       other than the obvious

I can destroy your image
  with a well-respected teacher/mentor

from the past
                     and let you know via **Cc:**

one last twist of the blade
always such a tempting
emotional release   isn't it ?

odd; aggressive
  plea for sympathy
under the guise of night
    and in the dim lights of ***"Hello!"***

odd; aggressive
the human race

and a naturally false
    thread
        in all

you've written yourself o u   t
of the potential immortality
        in the **word**

(and I've no respect for that)

so
all will disappear
as dust and bone
        forever an altar to impermanence

the bones of Siddhartha
 in a tower so tall
    on
        chan
         8
    you
      kiss
        the
       marble
   floor
     at
        eye
    level
before you see an apex there

        [I do not pretend to possess
          any qualities of enlightenment.
        I am no Buddha. There is no
           Buddhahood within me.]

and with meaning amongst the rubble
of human resolve

are
remains as   aftermath -
         an unsolicited attack

letters and sentence fragments
     e   v   e   r y   wh er   e
at the gates
 and in the walls

the bones of Siddhartha
are indifferent to
the ill wills of man

odd; aggressive
the human race

this will be the last time
I politely ask you
to remove **ME**

from
further communications

forever
as I meditate
and focus

> *[I do not pretend to possess*
> *   any qualities of enlightenment.*
> *I am no Buddha. There is no*
> *   Buddhahood within me.]*

alone and happy
away from

odd; aggressive
the human race

- MLE KW '17

Northern
A   State on the   Border
Southern

Dictators
Soldiers
Police
and
Politicians

Choose wisely,
Son.my baby
my Sun.

They are attacking
everyone, in the streets
tonight

breaking windows
burning buildings

finally, some passion
misplaced
but—

passion nonetheless.

I have chosen violence
I hate it here
and

I miss home.

Sometimes people speak
on the street, at night

under streetlights

and sometimes
people die
there

for no good reason.

It's hard at times
to find your crowd
when everyone
has a Cause
to die for.

religion, rage, and raw materials

Choose wisely,
Son.my baby
my Sun.

It's basically a
southern state on
the northern border.

> *Writers*
> *Painters*
> *Poets*
> *and*
> *Pessimists*

*"I hate it there, but
the cost of living is low." -SB/ME*

Life10: For Nosferatu-950
from the Road

That Damned Yankee
called again

from the road

reminded me
heading east

at 100mph:

jackrabbits are killers
and tumbleweeds are distractions

stacked against midwestern
fence lines that parallel
indiscriminate
farm lands—

"If you travel and you can't get back to me, it's OK. But, I ain't heard from you here in quite awhile. And, I think I can talk to you for a few minutes this time. So, why don't you give me a call when you get the chance? Don't wait a minute on life. Wish you were here. Glad you aren't."

Be seeing you

again, in time,
    Life10.

Respect. Salute.
Love. Honor.
                  -ME Out

The Immortal Nos-950

[Post-Flight]

Closing Thoughts

I had a dream about you last night — you bought a house Bob Dylan used to live in; you invited a ton of people to stay over and while we did not speak, you knew I was there and I knew it didn't matter if we talked.

>You knew. You always know
>It didn't matter. Like a rolling stone
>I was traveling home last night,
>listening to Bob Dylan.

>You were there. We did not speak
>It didn't matter. Like a completeunknown
>When it was all over
>I fell asleep
>with the windows open
>and the glow of neon light
>On my face.

From A Dying Breed

I don't believe in a lot of things,
> but I do believe in quantum entanglement.

Sent from Undisclosed Location by A-3104.ME

Escape Velocity

www.ingramcontent.com/pod-product-compliance
Lightning Source LLC
Chambersburg PA
CBHW021858230426
43671CB00006B/444